Meditations for

Inner Peace

JUST A MINUTE

Meditations for
Inner Peace

By Kathryn J. Hermes, FSP

Pauline
BOOKS & MEDIA
Boston

Library of Congress Cataloging-in-Publication Data

Names: Hermes, Kathryn, author.

Title: Meditations for inner peace / by Kathryn J. Hermes, FSP.

Description: Boston, MA : Pauline Books & Media, 2018. | "This book has been excerpted from Cherished by the Lord (Pauline Books & Media, 2012)."

Identifiers: LCCN 2018021773| ISBN 9780819849823 (pbk.) | ISBN 0819849820

Subjects: LCSH: Bible--Meditations.

Classification: LCC BS491.5 .H46 2018 | DDC 242/.2--dc23

LC record available at https://lccn.loc.gov/2018021773

Unless otherwise noted, the Scripture quotations contained herein are from the *New Revised Standard Version Bible: Catholic Edition,* copyright © 1989, 1993, Division of Christian Education of the National Council of the Churches of Christ in the United States of America. Used by permission. All rights reserved.

Other Scripture texts in this work are taken from the *New American Bible, Revised Edition* © 2010, 1991, 1986, 1970, Confraternity of Christian Doctrine, Washington, D.C., and are used by permission of the copyright owner. All Rights Reserved. No part of the *New American Bible* may be reproduced in any form without permission in writing from the copyright owner.

This book has been excerpted from *Cherished by the Lord* (Pauline Books & Media, 2012).

Cover design by Rosana Usselmann

Published by Pauline Books & Media, 50 Saint Pauls Avenue, Boston, MA 02130-3491. www.pauline.org

Printed in the U.S.A.

Pauline Books & Media is the publishing house of the Daughters of St. Paul, an international congregation of women religious serving the Church with the communications media.

1 2 3 4 5 6 7 8 9   22 21 20 19 18

Introduction

Has anyone ever smiled at you so radiantly that you felt they were saying, "I'm *delighted* you are here!"? At least once in a lifetime we each should receive that gift! When someone says to us that they are glad we exist, our heart leaps and we feel at home. Because we rarely receive the message that such a smile brings, we suffer. We conclude that no one really wants us as a friend or considers us of value. Life's trials, temptations, and tragedies threaten to rob us of our inner peace and to drown us in darkness.

God has smiled upon us since creation. These meditations are a simple support to help you lift your eyes to the face of the One who loves you more than you could ever imagine. As you pray with them day after day, you will discover how God wants you to be content, as content as a baby in its mother's arms. Each meditation is carefully chosen to amaze you with what God has done for you in his gracious and marvelous act of redemption.

So here is an easy method of reading these meditations that I use. It will unlock in your heart the courage to believe in God's desire to save and bless you in all things:

1. God will lead you to be interested in certain meditations. Go wherever God leads you. You don't have to read these in order unless you'd like to.

2. Before you read, stop and remember a moment when someone delighted in having you around. Tell God how grateful you are for that gift of love.

3. Begin to read the meditation. Relish what you read. Notice the words and phrases that seem to light a fire that warms your heart. Enjoy the safety and beauty of that moment.

4. Talk to God about what is burdening you right now. Then reread the words of Scripture in the meditation, hearing them as if God were speaking to you by name. Even place your name right in the passage and imagine God speaking these words to you directly. Notice what it is like and tell God how grateful you are.

My desire for you is that you will bask in God's gaze as it rests upon you, that you will find calm and quiet for your soul, and will be content as a small child to sleep in his care for you.

Do Not Be Troubled

"Do not let your hearts be troubled. Believe in God, believe also in me. In my Father's house there are many dwelling places. If it were not so, would I have told you that I go to prepare a place for you? And if I go and prepare a place for you, I will come again and will take you to myself, so that where I am, there you may be also. And you know the way to the place where I am going." Thomas said to him, "Lord, we do not know where you are going. How can we know the way?" Jesus said to him, "I am the way, and the truth, and the life."

JN 14:1–6

• • • •

Divine revelation manifests God's glory. Jesus discloses to us the Father's glory and we are entranced by what we see: his goodness, his wisdom, his healing love. When we enter into the story of Jesus, it absorbs us and we come to know the God who is love revealed in Jesus his Son. The Holy

Spirit, sent by Jesus, blows through salvation history, making the life, death, and resurrection of Jesus alive in each age of the Church. Through the Spirit, Jesus reveals to each of us today the utter truth of God's glory. In doing so he reveals to us our own glory. He is the way to become good, as God is good, not through our own efforts but because God sent his Son to do what we could not. Jesus alone can stand before God as good, because he became flesh and died for us. Incorporated into Jesus through Baptism, we become sons and daughters of the Father, fountain of life and love. In and through Jesus, we stand before the Father as good.

Jesus, Master, Way, Truth, and Life, draw my heart to the true, the good, and the beautiful, that I might be taken up into the greatness of your Father's plan which wildly exceeds all I could dream or imagine.

An Extraordinary Mercy

Sing to the LORD a new song,
>   his praise in the assembly of the faithful.
Let Israel be glad in its maker,
>   the people of Zion rejoice in their king.
Let them praise his name in dance,
>   make music with tambourine and lyre.
For the LORD takes delight in his people,
>   honors the poor with victory.

>   Ps 149:1–4 (NABRE)

— · ◆ · · · ◆ · —

God loves us as if we were the center of his universe! We who have died and risen with Christ, we in whom the Son abides, we for whom Jesus answered to his Father with his life and with his death—we are the object of God's delight. We are chosen by God. Jesus spent his thirty-three years of life serving our needs with his own hands, wiping up our mess with his own blood, opening our future with his own death. God makes the impossible, possible; the unbelievable, reality.

What is unlovable will melt in his hands. What is ostentatious will thrill to be a cascade of lilies in a blooming field, clothed only with the brilliance God gives them. What is afraid will stand with the certainty of the resurrection. We shy away from grandeur and expectations, but we are drawn with confidence by this extraordinary mercy that will delight us eternally.

O Love! You wash my feet and tend to my vulnerability every day! Give me eyes to see you.

Undeserved Blessings

"For the kingdom of heaven is like a landowner who went out early in the morning to hire laborers for his vineyard. After agreeing with the laborers for the usual daily wage, he sent them into his vineyard. . . . When those hired about five o'clock came, each of them received the usual daily wage. Now when the first came, they thought they would receive more; but each of them also received the usual daily wage. And when they received it, they grumbled against the landowner. . . . But he replied to one of them, 'Friend, I am doing you no wrong; did you not agree with me for the usual daily wage? . . . Or are you envious because I am generous?'"

Mt 20:1–2, 9–11, 13, 15

——— ◆ • ◆ ———

In your Christian life, what do you consider your "daily wage"? Someone once asked what we would do if we met Hitler in heaven. The person next to me answered immediately, "He won't be in heaven! He can't be. I've been good my whole life, he shouldn't get the same reward as I get!" We don't know if

Hitler repented or not. The Gospel teaches that we must repent of our sins in order to be saved. The way we live our life matters! But this person saw heaven as the "wages" she would receive after doing good to others and keeping the commandments. She was entitled to heaven. She had a certain point, because Scripture also says, "For God is not unjust; he will not overlook your work and the love that you showed for his sake in serving the saints" (Heb 6:10). But our ability to gain that reward is itself a gift of God. This parable strikes to the heart of being Christian in today's culture of entitlement. We are owed nothing. It is a privilege that we know the commandments and have experienced the joy of being and doing for others in the spirit of Christ. In this parable, the grumbling workers miss the point entirely. Their attitude is, "God *owes* me." Jesus was teaching them to realize instead, "God *loves* me." In the ecstasy of that love they need do nothing but rejoice that others are given a share in it, even if they have done little or nothing to deserve it.

Jesus, help me to rejoice when others are blessed undeservedly. Help me know that I have been blessed undeservedly. Change my heart!

Bursting with Good News

Then his father Zechariah was filled with the
Holy Spirit and spoke this prophecy:
> "Blessed be the Lord God of Israel,
>> for he has looked favorably on his
>> people
>>> and redeemed them.
> He has raised up a mighty savior for us
>> in the house of his servant David. . . .
> By the tender mercy of our God,
>> the dawn from on high will break upon
>> us,
> to give light to those who sit in darkness
> and in the shadow of death,
>> to guide our feet into the way of peace."

Lk 1:67–69, 78–79

— • · · · • —

Prophecy and good news fill the first two chapters of Luke. Mary visits her cousin Elizabeth
and greets her, bursting with God's good news for
herself and for the world. With his tongue loosed

by his ultimate obedience, Zechariah blesses the Lord who has visited his people to set them free. God chose Zechariah's son to prepare the way for our salvation. The angels announce the birth of the Savior, calling the littlest and most unimportant people, the shepherds, to come in awe and wonder to see for themselves. People scurry about, celebrating the tidings of great joy. Sounds like Christmas! Zechariah, Mary, the angels, and the shepherds not only teach us how to celebrate Christmas, but how to live as Christian disciples. We have good news for our families and for our world. Are we too bursting with joy over this good news from God? As Christians we are ennobled, lifted up, glorified, divinized because of what Zechariah proclaims: God has set the power of salvation in the center of our lives. Nothing is more wonderful than this God who has come to be with us.

Lord, I get so lost in the labyrinth of my thoughts—in patterns of competition, self-importance, and cynicism. May the dawn from on high bring lightness to my step and your joy to my life.

A New Name

Then Abram fell on his face; and God said to him, "As for me, this is my covenant with you: You shall be the ancestor of a multitude of nations. No longer shall your name be Abram, but your name shall be Abraham; for I have made you the ancestor of a multitude of nations. I will make you exceedingly fruitful; and I will make nations of you, and kings shall come from you. I will establish my covenant between me and you, and your offspring after you throughout their generations, for an everlasting covenant, to be God to you and to your offspring after you."

Gen 17:3–7

• • • •

Once when riding a bus I began to notice the ads, storefronts, billboards, and people carrying bags boasting logos and Internet addresses. Suddenly I felt as though everything around me was screaming: "Buy me! Buy me! Buy me!" I felt like my identity had been reduced to that of a faceless consumer as various companies vied for my money. God's words to Abraham, however, point out to us that we are more than our spending power. We are persons who are in covenant with God. In this covenant we discover what it means to be *truly* human: sought out by God, loved, embraced, committed to by the One who was, who is, and who ever will be. This covenant assures us postmoderns that the identity we so desperately seek is found, not in designer clothes and plush waterfront homes, but in the arms of a loving God who can't abandon us.

My Lord, I hunger so much to know my life has meaning. Is it too much to ask you to call me by a new name? Tell me who you've created me to be.

Keep Your Eyes Open

Let love be genuine; hate what is evil, hold fast to what is good; love one another with mutual affection; outdo one another in showing honor. Do not lag in zeal, be ardent in spirit, serve the Lord. Rejoice in hope, be patient in suffering, persevere in prayer.

ROM 12:9–12

⬩ ⋯ ⬩

In autumn, the colorful array of changing leaves outside my office window turns into winter's barren bleakness, symbolic of what often happens to our spirits. We live a spiritual rhythm of ups and downs, fullness and barrenness, blossom and decay. The downs pave the way for the ups; barrenness creates the possibility of refilling; times of decay fertilize the new blossoms in our lives. When Saint Paul says, "Be ardent in spirit," he is no doubt referring to this ongoing cycle of life and death. But I believe he is thinking of something more. I often open books at random and spot read. I once came across this definition of prayer in *Teresa of Ávila—God Alone Suffices*: "To pray is to think of Jesus while loving him." It was as if a fire had been kindled within me. Those simple words ignited my brittle spirit into an ardent fire that burned away bad habits and replaced them with a yearning for holiness. It is the Holy Spirit who ignites these spiritual fires that make us long for more. Paul knew this, because the Spirit had transformed his ways of thinking, acting, and loving, making him a new creature in Christ. So keep your eyes open. The Spirit will use something in your everyday experience to ignite your spirit and inflame your heart.

Holy Spirit, stir up the ashes of my life and relight my inner fire. Amen.

Wordlessly Embrace His Feet

After the Sabbath, as the first day of the week was dawning, Mary Magdalene and the other Mary came to see the tomb . . . the angel said . . . "Then go quickly and tell his disciples, 'He has been raised from the dead, and he is going before you to Galilee; there you will see him. . . .'" Then they went away quickly from the tomb, fearful yet overjoyed, and ran to announce this to his disciples. And behold, Jesus met them on their way and greeted them. They approached, embraced his feet, and did him homage. Then Jesus said to them, "Do not be afraid. Go tell my brothers to go to Galilee, and there they will see me."

MT 28:1, 5, 7–10 (NABRE)

* · * · *

The image of prayer found in this Gospel passage speaks to me in a particular way. The women were seeking among the dead the One whom they loved. But suddenly they bump into the

Lord who was deliberately crossing their path. Jesus' death had shattered the world of his first followers. I can imagine the news of the crucifixion passing quickly from one disciple to another: the hushed suspense, the quiet agony, the shock, the fear, the sorrow. Then suddenly, less than three days later, they literally run into him, alive. Jesus must have stood there with exquisite tenderness, his heart full of compassion for their sorrow. I wonder if they stopped to notice the kindness in his eyes, for they were already bowed in adoration, blessing the ground upon which their Lord walked. When I find it difficult to pray, I join the women on the morning of the resurrection, and from the roots of my being, I adore. Wordlessly, I embrace his feet. Or I stop to notice the way Jesus looks at me, what his eyes say. If that is all we do when we pray, it is enough.

You are alive! You are here! You are my life's path! You are the way! You meet me every day! Jesus, Risen One, I adore you.

God Saves What He Has Made

But you, O Lord, are enthroned forever;
    your name endures to all generations.
You will rise up and have compassion on Zion,
    for it is time to favor it;
    the appointed time has come. . . .
The nations will fear the name of the Lord,
    and all the kings of the earth your glory.
For the Lord will build up Zion;
    he will appear in his glory.
He will regard the prayer of the destitute,
    and will not despise their prayer.

Ps 102:12–13, 15–17

—•••—

God reaches out to the people who are his beloved. Through the prophets, God tells them that their choice to love and follow other gods is a serious offense to their relationship with him. Now an incurable wound, an injury past healing, stands between them and God. Nevertheless, God promises to restore the relationship. *Look at this*, God says, *I shall restore you. When you return to your land you will rejoice with thanksgiving. Songs of joy will replace your tears, and happiness will fill your houses.* God manifests his glory to his people by saving them, by restoring the relationship they have chosen to sever by disowning him. God manifests himself as the supreme sovereign, the king of glory. But God's sovereignty is not ruthless power, a selfish subjugation of everyone and everything to his own desires and ambitions. God is above our petty power plays and greater than our rejection of his love. God is love. God cannot be nor do anything except love. The whole universe is full of his mighty deeds. He manifests the splendor of his majesty by reaching out and saving what he has made. The Father transfigures and transforms us into images of his Son so that we too might participate in his glory for all eternity.

Transfigure and transform me in you, Jesus. Fill me with the radiance of God. Amen.

Love Extravagantly

Six days before the Passover Jesus came to Bethany, the home of Lazarus, whom he had raised from the dead. There they gave a dinner for him. Martha served, and Lazarus was one of those at the table with him. Mary took a pound of costly perfume made of pure nard, anointed Jesus' feet, and wiped them with her hair. The house was filled with the fragrance of the perfume.

Jn 12:1–3

———•·•·•———

I had just finished a whirlwind project under a tight deadline. When that happens I almost always end up, to my embarrassment, talking too hastily, exaggerating, and pontificating. The project sucks me out of the space inside my spirit where I offer quiet hospitality to Jesus. I look everywhere except into the Lord's quiet eyes. In this Gospel, silence fills the home of Lazarus. He and his two sisters welcome Jesus, pay attention to him, serve him. None of them say a word. In fact, Jesus defends the extravagance of their love for him. Others in the scene speak harsh and violent words—they have taken their eyes off Jesus and have started looking in the other directions of their hearts' distorted desires.

Jesus, keep my eyes on you. Even in the whirlwind of daily activities help me grab onto you more tightly, serving you and pouring out the oil of my love for you in your Church.

Our Deepest Longings

Long ago God spoke to our ancestors in many and various ways by the prophets, but in these last days he has spoken to us by a Son, whom he appointed heir of all things, through whom he also created the worlds. He is the reflection of God's glory and the exact imprint of God's very being, and he sustains all things by his powerful word. When he had made purification for sins, he sat down at the right hand of the Majesty on high, having become as much superior to angels as the name he has inherited is more excellent than theirs.

Heb 1:1–4

• ◦ • • ◦ •

In this passage from Hebrews, Christ, whom angels glorified, shepherds adored, and kings honored, is presented to us. Who is this Christ? What does he mean for me? This Christ, this Son of God, is the answer to our deepest longings to know that we are loved, that our lives have meaning, that we have a future and that it is good. From the quiet Galilean hills explode a hope, a promise, a guarantee. Christ our high priest has been weighed down with our sins, our pains, our illnesses, and our tears. He has borne them all. He has died and all this has died with him. Christ has risen, and we too rise with him. He has conquered evil and death. We see our future in his triumph over death and in his ascension to the Father's right hand. In him we are taken into the circle of life and love within the Trinity. We are held and embraced there, hidden and protected. Such awe! God "has spoken to us. . . . When [his Son] had made purification for sins, he sat down at the right hand of the Majesty on high." He lives and so *we* will live forever.

Jesus, you live and so I will live! Forever! Amen.

His Gracious Act
of Redemption

O LORD, my heart is not lifted up,
    my eyes are not raised too high;
I do not occupy myself with things
    too great and too marvelous for me.
But I have calmed and quieted my soul,
    like a weaned child with its mother;
    my soul is like the weaned child that is
      with me.
O Israel, hope in the LORD
    from this time on and forevermore.

Ps 131

＊ ・ ・ ・ ＊

God wants us to be content, as content as a baby in its mother's arms. But in our life today this often seems like a pipe dream. A contented child in its mother's arms feels safe. Contentment also means being completely satisfied, with no need to look for anything else. A contented baby isn't reaching out for diversion or entertainment. A quiet child isn't squirming to get out of its mother's arms to go running off down the street. As adults, however, contentment doesn't come so easily. We no longer experience personal, financial, or even national security. Each new release of a digital gadget restarts the itch of wanting more things until we have decided whether or not to purchase it. Many of us don't particularly like the role that is ours in the world: it might be too small, too tight, too hectic, too heavy. We cast around for something else that seems like a better fit. Psalm 131 offers us a secret for contentment: look to God and not to yourself. See what God has done in his gracious and marvelous act of redemption. Renounce any source of significance or security other than God.

O God, I have calmed and quieted my soul, content with all you give me, asleep in your care for me.

How Could We Fear?

I will make a covenant of peace with them; it shall be an everlasting covenant with them; and I will bless them and multiply them, and will set my sanctuary among them forevermore. My dwelling place shall be with them; and I will be their God, and they shall be my people. Then the nations shall know that I the LORD sanctify Israel, when my sanctuary is among them forevermore.

EZEK 37:26–28

◆·•·◆

With its mounting joy and jubilant hope for an eternal covenant, this passage contrasts with the seeming darkness and threat of death in the final chapters of the Gospels. There we read about the way Jesus established the New Covenant. What went wrong? Or perhaps we should ask what went right, that this covenant promised through the centuries should be written in the blood of the Son of God? The passion and death of Jesus shows us the extent God goes to in establishing this covenant that sets us free to love him and to live entirely for him. God the Father poured out all his love for us when he sent his Son to become one of us. The Son poured out all his love for us when he became as vulnerable and obedient as a "lamb that is led to the slaughter" (Isa 53:7). With us and for us he experienced and defeated our greatest enemy: death. Since Pentecost the Holy Spirit has been poured out in love on us, as a promise and guarantee that this covenant can never be broken. Humanity was unable to keep its part of the eternal covenant. So God himself, in Jesus, has kept our side of the covenant for us. What a love. *What a love!* God himself did what we could not do ourselves. How could we fear anything from such a love?

Such a love! Jesus, I trust in you!

We're Beloved, Desired, Died For

"To the Lᴏʀᴅ our God belongs justice; to us, people of Judah and inhabitants of Jerusalem, to be shamefaced, as on this day—to us, our kings, rulers, priests, and prophets, and our ancestors. We have sinned in the Lᴏʀᴅ's sight and disobeyed him. We have not listened to the voice of the Lᴏʀᴅ, our God, so as to follow the precepts the Lᴏʀᴅ set before us. From the day the Lᴏʀᴅ led our ancestors out of the land of Egypt until the present day, we have been disobedient to the Lᴏʀᴅ, our God, and neglected to listen to his voice."

Bᴀʀ 1:15–19 (NABRE)

———•—◆—•———

This passage may cause some nervous shifting in the pews. *Why do these uncomfortable readings keep showing up? Let's hear again the story of the lilies of the field.* Indeed, taken in isolation, this passage on the justice of God can seem overly harsh. No passage of Scripture, however, can be separated from the whole. It has been said that if the Song of Songs were the only book of Scripture, we would have all we need to understand God and salvation history. The conjugal imagery of the lover's desire for the beloved in this short, unpretentious book of love-poems, unlocks the meaning of the rest of the Bible, and of this passage in particular. Why are we "shamefaced"? Why does Jesus mourn over us as he did over the cities that had witnessed his miracles and power? Because we have been *beloved*, courted, desired, died for. We have clung to pennies when God wanted to make us millionaires. The impassioned divine Lover would have us be the darling of his heart. This passage is not an angry invective, but the words of broken hearts—both human and divine. These hearts that desire love will not rest until they are loved and have proven their love to each other.

What can I do to prove my love for you, O everlasting Love!

By Grace We Are Saved

But God, who is rich in mercy, out of the great love with which he loved us even when we were dead through our trespasses, made us alive together with Christ—by grace you have been saved—and raised us up with him and seated us with him in the heavenly places in Christ Jesus, so that in the ages to come he might show the immeasurable riches of his grace in kindness toward us in Christ Jesus. For by grace you have been saved through faith, and this is not your own doing; it is the gift of God. . . . For we are what he has made us, created in Christ Jesus for good works, which God prepared beforehand to be our way of life.

EPH 2:4–8, 10

✦ · ✦ · ✦

God has already destined certain works to be an important part of the Christian life. How do we discover what they are? We could do so many good things; how do we know the specific deeds

God desires most of us? This passage from the Letter to the Ephesians gives us clues. Words such as "rich in mercy," "out of the great love with which he loved us," and "by grace you have been saved" tip us off. God has planned a tremendous work of art for humanity and civilization. This artistic creation is a direct reflection of God's love and life. It is that simple. The Father, from all eternity, loved the Son. In returning that love to the Father, they breathed forth the Holy Spirit. The Son, sent by the Father, turned around and gave that love away instead of holding on to it (see Phil 2:5-6). He emptied himself, became a man, walked among us, lived our life, and died our death, so that, as the Father had done, he could pour himself out in love for us who needed salvation. By grace we are saved. The deeds God desires of us are self-emptying acts of service of others, love to the point of giving our lives for one another.

Jesus, make my life a work of art. May I love others with a faithful love that seeks their good before my own.

An Ongoing Conversation

O that you would tear open the heavens and
come down,
> so that the mountains would quake at your
> presence....
When you did awesome deeds that we did not
expect,
> you came down, the mountains quaked at
> your presence....
Yet, O LORD, you are our Father;
> we are the clay, and you are our potter;
> we are all the work of your hand.

> ISA 64:1, 3, 8

One of my favorite images of God is that of a
gardener, or a potter. Not being a gardener
myself, when I plant something I dig a hole in the
dirt and put the plant in its new home. The end. I
don't weed, care for it, or water it. Once, my mother
took us kids to a ceramics class. It was okay, but as
soon as we finished, my interest dropped. I wasn't

invested in creating things. God, however, as gardener or potter, is deeply invested in what he creates. The image of potter is often portrayed as an image of power: God chooses how to shape the clay. For me the image of potter is intimately one with the image of God pouring himself into his creation. It is an image of love. I can hear God listening closely to everything we say as he shapes our lives. The shaping of the vessel is part of an ongoing conversation of love between potter and clay. On a particularly busy day, I (the clay) may tell God (the potter) that I am tired. I need help. God delights to bend over the little vessel he is loving into being and to care for me.

Listen closely, God, to the whisper of my heart. Bend over your creature, here, and let me know your ever tender love.

Held As a Child

Bless the LORD, O my soul,
 and all that is within me,
  bless his holy name.
Bless the LORD, O my soul,
  and do not forget all his benefits—
who forgives all your iniquity,
 who heals all your diseases,
who redeems your life from the Pit,
  who crowns you with steadfast love and
   mercy,
who satisfies you with good as long as you live
  so that your youth is renewed like the
   eagle's. . . .
  The LORD has compassion for those who
   fear him.
For he knows how we were made;
 he remembers that we are dust.

Ps 103:1–5, 13b–14

⋅—⋅ ⋅ ⋅ ⋅—⋅

I have a friend whose heart was broken in a failed relationship. He had trusted. He had hoped. He had loved. He had dreamed. In the end, his love was betrayed. I watched with wonder and compassion as he suffered and, in the pain, was transformed. Psalm 103 unfolded before me in the path he took during the years that followed his separation and divorce. He struggled with his own contribution to the failed relationship. However, God wasn't interested in focusing only on that. God calls us to repentance and renewal so that we may grow. God delights in us too much to let our relationship with him get stuck in fault-finding. Those who open their hearts to God in these pained life situations find their youth renewed much like the eagle who molts. The first lines of Psalm 103 outline the way God transforms us: he forgives our iniquity, heals our disease, crowns us with love and mercy, crowns us, satisfies us, and renews us like the eagle.

God, you know we are dust and unable to struggle through life's issues alone. Hold us as a child, nourished and secure in its mother's womb, renewing us over and over again, giving us new life and a new future. Amen.

Creative Generosity

Then I saw a new heaven and a new earth; for
the first heaven and the first earth had passed
away, and the sea was no more. . . . And I heard a
loud voice from the throne saying,
"See, the home of God is among mortals.
He will dwell with them;
they will be his peoples,
and God himself will be with them;
he will wipe every tear from their eyes.
Death will be no more;
mourning and crying and pain will be no more,
for the first things have passed away."

And the one who was seated on the throne
said, "See, I am making all things new."

REV 21:1, 3–5

—•·•·•—

God has intervened in human history. First, he
created us. Then he called the patriarch
Abraham, the father of the Chosen People. He rescued his people from Egypt through Moses. In

David, he provided for his people a king after his own heart. God himself came and lived among us in Jesus, Son of Mary and Son of God. Through his death, resurrection, and ascension, Jesus reconciled us with his Father. He is now seated at God's right hand, where we also hope to be one day. Just as an adult loves to surprise a child with a new gift or opportunity, God's delight is to do something new for us. Have you experienced anything unexpected from God lately? If we reflect on all the ways God has come to live in our neighborhood, mysteries that we celebrate annually in the liturgical feasts of Christmas, Holy Thursday, Good Friday, and Easter, we know that something new and unexpected has been given to us. Because Jesus has transformed us, *we* are that newness. We have been given a new identity because God interrupted human history with his love. For all eternity, we will be inundated with wave upon wave of God's creative generosity toward us.

Interrupt my life, Father, Son, and Spirit, and do something new!

An Immense Love

For I am about to create new heavens
    and a new earth;
the former things shall not be remembered
    or come to mind.
But be glad and rejoice for ever
    in what I am creating;
for I am about to create Jerusalem as a joy,
    and its people as a delight.
I will rejoice in Jerusalem,
    and delight in my people;
no more shall the sound of weeping be heard
  in it,
    or the cry of distress.

Isa 65:17–19

I n this passage, we are forced to stop and face the overwhelming, magnificent message of redemption: God is doing something new! It's not that God made a mistake at first. It's not that we had botched things up so badly that God decided to scrap everything and begin again with new people. Isaiah instead is painting a vision of love that has grown so immense it can create life, hope, and a future even in the midst of mistakes, sin, and death. This compassion is so divine that it straightens bent limbs, raises dead bodies and spirits, and transforms the dull and callous of heart. God will stop at nothing to make right our erring ways. He doesn't need to start over. Yesterday I saw a brave flower poking up through a crack in the sidewalk. The divine Lover is like this. Nothing can get in his way. He is unstoppable, for he has in mind to create something new of your life and mine.

Yes, Lord! Don't stop! Don't let me block your way! Do all that you desire to accomplish in my life!

Sought Out by God

For in him all the fullness of God was pleased to dwell, and through him God was pleased to reconcile to himself all things, whether on earth or in heaven, by making peace through the blood of his cross. And you who were once estranged and hostile in mind, doing evil deeds, he has now reconciled in his fleshly body through death, so as to present you holy and blameless and irreproachable before him—provided that you continue securely established and steadfast in the faith, without shifting from the hope promised by the gospel that you heard, which has been proclaimed to every creature under heaven.

Col 1:19–23

Recently I realized something about myself: I tend to make everything a project, and, true to form, I make my relationship with God a project too. It may seem like a good thing to be intent on growing in relationship with God. And it is true that my growing friendship with God hinges in part on the interest, love, and presence that God and I show each other. But I often forget that Jesus himself *has accomplished* something that has created my "status" in this relationship. Before we were even born, humanity was reconciled to God, and through Baptism you and I got the full package deal. We are members of the family—premium membership, paid in full. We are children of God, and Jesus is bound and determined to present us to his Father holy and irreproachable at the end. Saint Paul knew this—for God had sought him out and dramatically changed the direction of his life. This life-changing God whom Paul preaches is our hope and our salvation!

Lord, when I'm sure that the tangled confusion of my life is irredeemable, remind me of my place in your family.

Washed Clean

Wash yourselves; make yourselves clean;
    remove the evil of your doings
    from before my eyes;
cease to do evil,
    learn to do good;
seek justice,
    rescue the oppressed,
defend the orphan,
    plead for the widow.
Come now, let us argue it out,
    says the LORD:
though your sins are like scarlet,
    they shall be like snow;
though they are red like crimson,
    they shall become like wool.

ISA 1:16–18

———— ⬩ • ⬩ ————

I have met many who have difficulty with confession. I too struggled with the sacrament of Reconciliation for years. The regular rotation of saying the same thing, hearing the same thing, and reciting the same penance seemed like a divine laundry service for my soul, rather than an intimate encounter with Jesus that gradually intensified my union with him. This Scripture passage uses words such as learn, seek, and plead to convey a sense of progressive growth that should be a part of this sacrament. These words have helped me make my peace with confession. In preparation, I ask Jesus, *What in my life most jeopardizes our relationship?* I never get the same answer. It is always an unexpected and often uncomfortable revelation of a part of my life God wants to heal. I begin my confession with this discovery and by describing what God has been doing recently in my life. God's revelation and activity help me bring into the light those areas of my life that he wants to make white as snow.

Lord, I hear the eagerness of your heart to wipe away my sins, to transform me more completely into your disciple. I join my eagerness to yours. Lead me into a more mature celebration of Reconciliation that I may live ever more passionately as your disciple.

A Humble Love

While I was on my way and approaching Damascus, about noon a great light from heaven suddenly shone about me. I fell to the ground and heard a voice saying to me, "Saul, Saul, why are you persecuting me?" I answered, "Who are you, Lord?" Then he said to me, "I am Jesus of Nazareth whom you are persecuting." Now those who were with me saw the light but did not hear the voice of the one who was speaking to me. I asked, "What am I to do, Lord?" The Lord said to me, "Get up and go to Damascus; there you will be told everything that has been assigned to you to do."

ACTS 22:6–10

—◆ · ◆ · ◆—

All of Saint Paul's teaching to his beloved Christian communities flows from this first hard lesson he learned from Jesus the Master: great ideas—no matter how much you can justify them or how righteous you think you are—are dangerous when they are pursued apart from dependence on God and humble membership in community. Paul was not a bad man. He thought he had things figured out: the Christians were too much of a threat with their crazy ideas about this dead man they claimed had risen. Jesus, however, showed himself to Paul as very much alive and intimately connected to a human community. Paul had to teach this lesson over and over to the first Christian communities, and we find it difficult to learn as well. All too often we are intransigent in our way of dealing with one another and assessing one another's viewpoints. People who claim they are better than others, more intelligent than others, more right than others, more righteous than others, have yet to learn the lesson of Pauline conversion: dependent faith and humble love, as together we are built up into community.

Paul, stopped in your tracks by the Lord, obtain for us a true conversion. May we too begin to truly know the joyful message of the Christian Gospel and be the Lord's witnesses to all the world.

Restored Relationships

Do not judge, and you will not be judged; do not condemn, and you will not be condemned. Forgive, and you will be forgiven; give, and it will be given to you. A good measure, pressed down, shaken together, running over, will be put into your lap; for the measure you give will be the measure you get back.

Lk 6:37–38

❖ ⋅ ⋅ ❖

Though I desire God to show me mercy, generosity, understanding, and forgiveness, there are times when I have a hard time extending this same liberality toward others. Why? Our judgments proceed from our beliefs. Beliefs can be a simple desire: "a good family eats together"; an erroneous idea: "Christians don't get angry"; a dangerous attitude: "people should not oppose me"; or a lifestyle choice: "a successful standard of living means we have two cars." Based on our beliefs we weigh others' behavior. Unless they are transformed by the Gospel, our beliefs lead to judgments that create disunity and pain. *Biblical judgment*, however, is not aimed at punishment but at restoring relationship. Here precisely is the rub. It is more satisfying and much easier to harshly condemn others from the perspective of unexamined beliefs. Every line in this Gospel selection, instead, is about relationship. We are called to analyze our beliefs, weigh them according to the criteria of the Gospel, correct some (probably many) of them, and focus on restoring relationships. Happiness flows from overcoming the human propensity to condemn others, and instead working generously to build up relationships with them.

Generous forgiveness and infinite mercy of God, flow through me into the lives of all.

Treat Me with Love

Who is a God like you, pardoning iniquity
    and passing over the transgression
    of the remnant of your possession?
He does not retain his anger forever,
    because he delights in showing clemency.
He will again have compassion upon us;
    he will tread our iniquities under foot.
You will cast all our sins
    into the depths of the sea.

MIC 7:18–19

———•—•—•———

This interesting image could be a bit misleading. It could give us the idea that our sins are objects distinct from us. By casting them into the sea we could conclude that they have no real impact on us or on our relationship with God. But from the Garden of Eden, to the Chosen People's rebellion against the Lord, to the Prodigal Son who takes his life into his own hands and turns his back on the Father, to the hill of Calvary, it is clear that how we deal with sin is deeply connected with who we become. In these biblical passages, sin is defined as a distorted desire to *break free* from divine prohibition, as a cynical belief that God's demands are *contrary* to our interests. Sound familiar? Any parent should recognize the characteristics of children who want to break away from their parent's authority. As spiritual children, we at times also choose this so-called freedom rather than acknowledge the Love that sustains our lives.

Lord, show me how short-sighted, self-interested, and self-indulgent I still am in parts of my life. Open my eyes to your true identity: Love, you who can only treat me with Love, and desire that I live wholly in Love.

Catch My Attention

In the beginning was the Word, and the Word was with God, and the Word was God. He was in the beginning with God. All things came into being through him, and without him not one thing came into being. What has come into being in him was life, and the life was the light of all people. The light shines in the darkness, and the darkness did not overcome it.

Jn 1:1–5

• • • •

This Gospel passage is about beginnings. God is good at beginnings. In the beginning the Spirit hovered over the waters and God created the world. In the beginning was the Word, and the Word was made flesh and took up residence among us. In the beginning of our Christian life we were baptized, immersed in the water to die and rise with Jesus. Creation. Redemption. Sanctification. In each case, the people God chose to bless with his beginnings promised fidelity to the covenant God made with them. In each case, including our own, we failed to keep our promises and chose something other than God as the center of our lives. And in each case, including our own, God was right there to set things right, to catch our attention and allure us back to relationship with him. Each day is a new beginning. Each day is another opportunity to discover God who is trying to attract and coax us to a greater love.

I am here, my Lord. I sense that you have something you want to say to me, something special you want to give me. I am ready. I am here. I am here for you.

Probe Our Hearts

Now in Jerusalem by the Sheep Gate there is a pool, called in Hebrew Beth-zatha, which has five porticoes. In these lay many invalids—blind, lame, and paralyzed. One man was there who had been ill for thirty-eight years. When Jesus saw him lying there and knew that he had been there a long time, he said to him, "Do you want to be made well?" The sick man answered him, "Sir, I have no one to put me into the pool when the water is stirred up; and while I am making my way, someone else steps down ahead of me." Jesus said to him, "Stand up, take your mat and walk."

JN 5:2–8

- - • • • - -

J esus is the master of asking the obvious! Who would walk into a hospital where someone has lain for two years in bed, chronically ill, too sick to go home, unresponsive to medical treatments, and ask, "Do you want to get better?" But Jesus did just that! For thirty-eight years this man had been in the portico by the pool waiting to be healed. So why did Jesus ask him what he wanted? Wasn't it obvious? Jesus was probing the man's heart with this simple inquiry. *What do you want?* he asked. Interestingly, the man didn't answer the question. He complained about not having anyone to help him into the water. Jesus cured the man and told him to go home. The man didn't ask to follow Jesus, didn't express gratitude, didn't show the genesis of anything greater in his life than that healing. Neither did Jesus invite the man to accompany him as a disciple. The man didn't know his heart well enough to really know what he wanted in life. And you, what do you most deeply desire for yourself? Your family? The world?

Sadly, my Lord, my heart sometimes lacks passion. At times I don't know what I truly want in life. Have mercy on me.

I Need You

Two men went up to the temple to pray, one a Pharisee and the other a tax collector. The Pharisee, standing by himself, was praying thus, "God, I thank you that I am not like other people: thieves, rogues, adulterers, or even like this tax collector. I fast twice a week; I give a tenth of all my income." But the tax collector, standing far off, would not even look up to heaven, but was beating his breast and saying, "God, be merciful to me, a sinner!" I tell you, this man went down to his home justified rather than the other; for all who exalt themselves will be humbled, but all who humble themselves will be exalted.

Lk 18:10–14

◆ ◆ ◆ ◆

This Gospel reading is like a film of Matthew's Beatitudes, in which Jesus declares *fortunate* those whose only recourse is God. Luke's parables are stories that can help us understand what Jesus means. We see the widow who cries out for legal justice, and the children who in their simplicity cry out for blessing. The rich official cries out for righteousness (though he goes away because he wants to hold on to his riches), and the blind man at Jericho cries out for his one great need: to see God. In this selection, we have the tax collector who mourns his sins and cries out for forgiveness. In this chapter, only the Pharisee, a good man and a strict observer of the Law, is not *fortunate*. The Pharisee saw no need to cry out, to reach out of himself and beg God for justice, blessing, mercy, or vision. The Pharisee didn't get it, because he felt he had in himself everything he wanted or needed. Jesus, instead, came for those who had no one but God to depend on. Do you need God yet? If you do, you are indeed *fortunate*.

I need you, my God. Accept my heart reaching out to you.

Feelings of Insecurity Frighten Me

At the approach of Saul and David, on David's return after striking down the Philistine, women came out from all the cities of Israel to meet Saul the king, singing and dancing, with tambourines, joyful songs, and stringed instruments. The women played and sang:

"Saul has slain his thousands,
and David his tens of thousands."

Saul was very angry and resentful of the song, for he thought: "They give David tens of thousands, but only thousands to me. All that remains for him is the kingship." From that day on, Saul kept a jealous eye on David.

1 Sm 18:6–9 (NABRE)

- - - - -

Sometimes just a word that highlights how someone else is better than we are can make our insecurity flare up. Especially when we are holding on to something that makes us feel good about our-selves, we can become very touchy and anxious when it is threatened. Basically *all* of us who travel together on this precarious journey we call life suffer from at least a mild case of insecurity. Once in a while we are reminded that what we hang on to for security could be taken away from us. We discover that the people we think we live in solidarity with are actually a threat. Both Saul and David were insecure. Both of them were holding on to the admiration of the crowds. Jonathan, King Saul's son, was a level-headed peacemaker because he wasn't holding on to anything. He was looking out for the good of both Saul and David. Neither his father nor his friend was a threat to him.

Jesus, feelings of insecurity frighten me. I don't like to feel anxious or jealous. When I feel threatened, send me a Jonathan. Amen.

Genuine Love

Now that you have purified your souls by your obedience to the truth so that you have genuine mutual love, love one another deeply from the heart. You have been born anew, not of perishable but of imperishable seed, through the living and enduring word of God. For

"All flesh is like grass
    and all its glory like the flower of grass.
The grass withers,
    and the flower falls,
    but the word of the Lord endures forever."

That word is the good news that was announced to you.

1 Pet 1:22–25

＊ ・ ・ ・ ＊

All of us have times when we just don't agree with others. We may see things differently because of our backgrounds, life experiences, personal agendas, and values. Once in a while, we have to admit, it's because of obstinacy. In his letter Peter says that we are purified so that we can experience genuine love of one another by *obedience to the truth*. This is such a freeing phrase. Obedience to the truth calls me to become a bigger person. It shapes in me a great heart, and it attracts me to the sacrifices that will create better character in me. To obey the truth we need four qualities: simplicity, sincerity, uprightness, and openness. We must be like a little child who is a bundle of wonder. Everything is new! Everything is full of awe and mystery! Such a child is open to all that is true. As adults we can recapture this sense of reverent wonder at what is coming to be, what the possibilities are, the gift of another's values, or the other side of the story. We can opt for the humility of listening, waiting, and asking.

Transform the smallness of my obstinate clinging to my point of view into a large-heartedness modeled after your heart, my God. Mellow me that I may give the gift of love to all I meet.

We Live in Christ

Now concerning the times and the seasons, brothers and sisters, you do not need to have anything written to you. For you yourselves know very well that the day of the Lord will come like a thief in the night. When they say, "There is peace and security," then sudden destruction will come upon them, as labor pains come upon a pregnant woman, and there will be no escape! But you, beloved, are not in darkness, for that day to surprise you like a thief; for you are all children of light and children of the day; we are not of the night or of darkness.

1 Thess 5:1–5

———— ·•·•· ————

This passage is exultant! Saint Paul reminds his beloved Thessalonians that they are now living in this world of light created by the Word. Jesus is the Word of God. His words divide light from darkness and create healing and wholeness. His words make things happen! Whether we are alive or have died—and this is the key to Paul and to our own lives—we live *in Christ*. We, individually and as a community, have actually *become* Christ. When the Father looks at us he sees his Son standing in our stead. This gives us hope in the midst of all our problems. We will never be alone! Jesus cares for each of us as if we were his very own self! We truly are. When times are dark, Jesus has not forgotten you. He can't forget you—ever. You are *in* him.

Glory be to you, O Father, creator of the day, maker of the light.

Our Utter Glory
Is Obedience

The people spoke against God and against
Moses, "Why have you brought us up out of
Egypt to die in the wilderness? For there is no
food and no water, and we detest this miserable
food." Then the LORD sent poisonous serpents
among the people, and they bit the people, so
that many Israelites died. The people came to
Moses and said, "We have sinned by speaking
against the LORD and against you; pray to the
LORD to take away the serpents from us." So
Moses prayed for the people. And the LORD said
to Moses, "Make a poisonous serpent, and set it
on a pole; and everyone who is bitten shall look
at it and live."

NUM 21:5–8

———— ◆ ··· ◆ ————

This has always been one of my favorite Scripture
passages. As I've grown older it has knit its way
into the fiber of my soul. As the people argued with

Moses that dry, dusty day, it wasn't the food and water that caused all the havoc with the snakes. It was the power of the people's wills and the direction they pointed them in that made all the difference. If our wills are pointed toward self, then we'll argue over something as small as a drink of water. We'll think of a hundred reasons to demand the water *now*. If our wills are pointed toward God, in the light of truth and goodness, and under God's authority, we discover freedom. We will receive glory even in the case of humiliation and failure. Our wills are always in relation to another's. *God* loved us, *God* sent his Son: we obey in freedom and love. If we can let go of our need to do things our way, we can discover a better way. It is the way that Jesus came to show us: obedience is the utter glory of the human creature.

Obedience can be a hard word, Lord, until I remember that you have led the way even in this. You, the obedient Son of the Father, have made all obedience fruitful. Help me to follow you. Amen.

We Are Powerless

After [Jesus] had finished speaking, he said to
Simon, "Put out into deep water and lower your
nets for a catch." Simon said in reply, "Master, we
have worked hard all night and have caught
nothing, but at your command I will lower the
nets." When they had done this, they caught a
great number of fish and their nets were tear-
ing. . . . When Simon Peter saw this, he fell at the
knees of Jesus and said, "Depart from me, Lord,
for I am a sinful man." Jesus said to Simon, "Do
not be afraid; from now on you will be catching
men."

Lk 5:4–6, 8, 10 (NABRE)

———•·•·•———

Poor Peter! He's just been overwhelmed by
God's magnificent generosity. Suddenly Peter
realized *who* is in his boat. It would be like a taxi
cab driver who stops at the scene of an accident and
sees his passenger miraculously bring someone
back from the dead. Whoa! When we witness a

remarkable display of God's presence and love, our first reaction is often to create distance. I think that's because such experiences make it clear to us on a very deep level that we are not as powerful as we think. Like Peter—the professional fisherman who couldn't force the fish into his net but discovered that someone else could fill his nets on command—we realize our smallness and poverty in the midst of a creation so vast it can't be controlled or explained. We are indeed powerless in the face of so many things in life. Jesus wants to work miracles for you, in your boat, where you live and work today—miracles that will help you see what he wants to do in your life and the mission he has given you. Stay awake!

Come, Jesus, into my boat. I long to be surprised by your generosity today. I long to witness the evidence of your care for me. Come!

Humility

My brothers and sisters, do you with your acts of favoritism really believe in our glorious Lord Jesus Christ? For if a person with gold rings and in fine clothes comes into your assembly, and if a poor person in dirty clothes also comes in, and if you take notice of the one wearing the fine clothes and say, "Have a seat here, please," while to the one who is poor you say, "Stand there," or, "Sit at my feet," have you not made distinctions among yourselves, and become judges with evil thoughts? For judgment will be without mercy to anyone who has shown no mercy; mercy triumphs over judgment.

JAS 2:1–4, 13

Recently I've learned how important it is to lay on the table what I know, or think I know, and allow it to be measured by the experiences and insights of others. The evil spirit plays a sneaky trick: convincing me I don't need others, leading me to protect myself by isolation, making me fear someone else's sharp mind, or to be defensive of my own way of Christian living. What starts out as fear ends as prejudice. This passage from James seems so blatant that it almost doesn't strike home. I would probably never speak to a poor person in the way James describes; poverty usually draws forth compassion. However, I would be wise to admit that I do think this way about people who threaten me or cause me anxiety. They are not financially poor, but, in my insecurity, I paint them as poor in virtue, poor in intelligence, poor in personal talent.

Lord, convince me of my poverty so that I can trust you entirely with my life. Free me from anxiety so that I can trust the gifts of others. Save me from prejudice so that together with others, I may seek you in humility and mutual love. Amen.

God's Love Saves Me!

For God so loved the world that he gave his only Son, so that everyone who believes in him may not perish but may have eternal life. Indeed, God did not send the Son into the world to condemn the world, but in order that the world might be saved through him. Those who believe in him are not condemned; but those who do not believe are condemned already, because they have not believed in the name of the only Son of God.

Jn 3:16–18

Experiencing a text is often the best way to get its meaning. Once on a retreat I experienced for the first time what the words of this passage mean. For the first readers of John's Gospel, the Greek word *sōzō*, meaning *to save*, had the powerful sense of deliverance from a particularly *perilous* situation, or from a mortal danger. Kneeling in chapel, after celebrating the sacrament of Reconciliation, I was overwhelmed with a knowledge from the inside out that I had been rescued, delivered, protected, that someone had grabbed my hand just as I was slipping away. I felt like I had been brought out of harm's way when I had no way to save myself. That is what Jesus is all about. God refused to give up on us. He handed over the dearest possession the Father has, his only Son, so that we would be brought up into God's embrace and lifted to a place of rest, love, belonging, and mercy.

God, you did not send your Son to definitively sever any friendship or responsibility you might have in our regard. No. You sent your Son to rescue us because you can do nothing less than remain faithful to your covenant of love forever.

Love Always Triumphs

Thus says the LORD:
I am going to restore the fortunes of the tents
  of Jacob,
      and have compassion on his dwellings. . . .
Their prince shall be one of their own,
      their ruler shall come from their midst;
I will bring him near, and he shall approach me,
      for who would otherwise dare to approach
        me?
          says the LORD.
And you shall be my people,
      and I will be your God.

JER 30:18, 21–22

———• · · · •———

Here the Lord makes an astonishing commitment of love! Astonishing because it is not promised to people who have proven themselves worthy of such recognition from God. Rather, Jeremiah had clearly stated that the peoples' sin was so grievous that their wound was incurable. They had no hope for healing, no relief in sight for their pain. Such cruel words could only come from a broken heart. Often Scripture portrays God as brokenhearted at the disloyalty of his people. He abandons them to their own devices and exile. But love, even when betrayed, still triumphs. "I am going to restore the fortunes of the tents of Jacob. . . ." No matter what we've done, no matter how awful the circumstances of our lives, which could even cause us to cry out against God, love will triumph. God will not let us go. We are his people and he is our God.

Do not let me go, my God. Hold on to me even when I would run away. Let your love conquer me! I claim you as my God, for you have claimed me as your child.

The Reason I'm Still Alive

The LORD is my shepherd, I shall not want.
> He makes me lie down in green pastures;
he leads me beside still waters;
> he restores my soul.
He leads me in right paths
> for his name's sake.
Even though I walk through the darkest valley,
> I fear no evil;
for you are with me;
> your rod and your staff—
> they comfort me.
. . . Surely goodness and mercy shall follow me
> all the days of my life,
and I shall dwell in the house of the LORD
> my whole life long.

Ps 23:1–4, 6

＊ ‧ ‧ ‧ ＊

I speak often with a mother, Sarah, whose husband turned her and their two girls out of their home in order to marry another woman. Sarah spent almost a year in homeless shelters with her children. Gradually she earned enough money to move to another town, find new schools for the girls, and buy a small house. Only one thing gets her out of bed in the morning—her children. Psalm 23 is one of her favorite psalms: *The Lord is my shepherd. . . . He leads me, he restores my soul, he gives me courage, he anoints me, and I shall live with him forever.* The psalmist declares his unshakeable faith in the love of God for him, "even though I walk through the darkest valley." Sarah has learned this lesson well. I am moved when she tells me how much God loves her. She knows it is only God who has helped her survive all she has been through: "He is the reason I am still alive." She declares her faith in him in the midst of the chaos. From the psalmist and from Sarah, I've learned that adoration and self-abandonment are the truly Christian response to the vicissitudes of our life journey.

I thank you, my Lord, for all those who witness to your fidelity as they walk through dark valleys. They are a gift to me.

Touching God's Presence

In the sixth month the angel Gabriel was sent by God to a town in Galilee called Nazareth, to a virgin engaged to a man whose name was Joseph, of the house of David. The virgin's name was Mary.... The angel said to her, "Do not be afraid, Mary, for you have found favor with God. And now, you will conceive in your womb and bear a son, and you will name him Jesus. He will be great, and will be called the Son of the Most High, and the Lord God will give to him the throne of his ancestor David. He will reign over the house of Jacob forever, and of his kingdom there will be no end."

LK 1:26–27, 30–33

◆ ◆ ◆ ◆

A woman once said to me, "You seem to be able to touch God's presence as if it were real." *AS IF it were real!* Without realizing it, she had put into words our modern anguish that God seems so remote. He seems to be nothing more than invisible gas—a ghostly non-reality, a deity without the face or voice we long to see and hear. This modern conception of God is far from the triune God, the Father whose Son became Mary's baby—personal, compassionate, involved, committed to us. This Gospel passage speaks of visions of angels, messages from God, commitments of faith, obedient adoration: things that can easily be brushed off as the uninformed piety of the simple minded. After all, science and technology claim to know what *really* makes the world go round. This Gospel, however, puts us squarely in the realm of the reality that only the faith of the simple can see. God is as real and involved in our lives as when he asked Mary to be the mother of his Son.

Mary, show us God's face once more. Teach us to hear his voice again and again. Amen.

A Tidal Wave of Love

And when they came to a place called Golgotha
(which means Place of a Skull), they offered him
wine to drink, mixed with gall; but when he
tasted it, he would not drink it. And when they
had crucified him, they divided his clothes
among themselves by casting lots; then they sat
down there and kept watch over him. Over his
head they put the charge against him, which
read, "This is Jesus, the King of the Jews." . . .
From noon on, darkness came over the whole
land until three in the afternoon. And about
three o'clock Jesus cried with a loud voice. . . .
"My God, my God, why have you forsaken
me?" . . . Then Jesus cried again with a loud voice
and breathed his last.

Mt 27:33–37, 45–46, 50

———•·•·•———

Crucified and forsaken on the Cross, Jesus
shows us to what great extent we are called to
love. He is the image of the divine dance of love in

the Trinity: it is total, all-embracing, completely self-forgetful, total gift. We cannot see the Persons of the Trinity in their relationships with one another. But we *can* see how Jesus, the Incarnate Son of God, has loved us. Jesus came and carried all the weight of our burden. He took upon himself not only our sin, but our death, our experience of frustrated relationships, our alienation, our forsakenness. He did not love us with a sterile love from afar. He touched us and held us. He nursed us back to health with the healing balm of his death and paid the price of our salvation with his own blood. What would happen if we loved one another this way? It is hard, I must admit. Efficiency, the bottom line, advantage, and personal plans have to give way and crumble before the onslaught of this tidal wave of love. But, oh, how much more blessed and fulfilled would our lives be? And the world? Would it not be a much more beautiful place to live?

From this point, Lord, I resolve to live a life of total, self-forgetful gift. May my love contribute to peace in the world.

Build Up the Body of Christ

For just as the body is one and has many members, and all the members of the body, though many, are one body, so it is with Christ. For in the one Spirit we were all baptized into one body—Jews or Greeks, slaves or free—and we were all made to drink of one Spirit. . . .

Now you are the body of Christ and individually members of it.

1 COR 12:12–13, 27

———•·•·•———

Together we are Christ in the world. Together. A tough word. It would be easier to do it one by one, individually, alone, on my own time, in my own style, to my own end. But we can't get away from that little word: together. We are all members of one body, and that body is Christ. This means that whenever one of us is present to another, Christ is present. When someone ministers to us, Christ is ministering. When I teach someone, Christ is teaching. We do not need to be afraid of conflicts. They are created by our struggles to grow in maturity and to overcome individualism, collectivism, isolation, and self-serving agendas. These conflicts sand away the sharp edges of our characters and transform our selfishness until the body can live together as one, in harmony, in mutual obedience, growing in love and freedom. Each of us is not simply a cell in the body of Christ. Each of us individually and together is Christ's body. Each of us can build up the body of Christ within ourselves, for the sake of others, in the Church and in service to the world.

How can it be that I—and each of us—have been raised to the honor of being members of the body of Christ? For this, Lord, I praise you.

Where to Look for Jesus

[O]n that same day two of them were going to a village called Emmaus, about seven miles from Jerusalem, and talking with each other about all these things that had happened. While they were talking and discussing, Jesus himself came near and went with them, but their eyes were kept from recognizing him.... Then he said to them, "Oh, how foolish you are, and how slow of heart to believe all that the prophets have declared!" Then beginning with Moses and all the prophets, he interpreted to them the things about himself in all the scriptures....

When he was at the table with them, he took bread, blessed and broke it, and gave it to them. Then their eyes were opened, and they recognized him....

LK 24:13–16, 25, 27, 30–31

—◆ · · · ◆—

It is such a grace that the Gospel of Luke gives us this account! Without it, how would we know where to look for Jesus? All that we read prior to the resurrection recounts people coming to Jesus when they could see him, hear him, and physically grasp his hand. But what about those of us who live after Jesus' ascension? How will we know where to find him? How can we hear him? Saint Luke's account of the two disciples teaches me three lessons about finding Jesus. First, on my own, like the two disciples, the best I can do is attempt to figure things out. Jesus meets me on the road I am walking. He will reveal to me a different way of seeing things: the way of faith. Second, Jesus tells me not to be afraid of the crises I or others experience. They will all, like the crucifixion, one day be mysteriously taken up and transfigured in a manner none of us can know right now. Third, we will find Jesus always, whenever we need him, in the breaking of the bread. Jesus left us the Eucharist so that he would be here with us always and we would be able to find him. And all this comes to us through the Church.

Jesus, our Life, come to meet us. When we are confused, lost, or discouraged, come alongside us. Draw us to the breaking of the bread.

Remembering the Promise

His divine power has given us everything needed for life and godliness, through the knowledge of him who called us by his own glory and goodness. Thus he has given us ... his precious and very great promises, so that through them you may escape from the corruption that is in the world because of lust, and may become participants of the divine nature. For this very reason, you must make every effort to support your faith with goodness, and goodness with knowledge, and knowledge with self-control, and self-control with endurance, and endurance with godliness, and godliness with mutual affection, and mutual affection with love. . . . For anyone who lacks these things is short-sighted and blind, and is forgetful of the cleansing of past sins.

2 Pet 1:3–7, 9

◆ · · · ◆

This passage is a kind of "scrapbook" that memorializes the various facets of our Christian life. Do you keep a "spiritual scrapbook"?

We can too quickly lose track of the "precious and very great promises" that we have received. These promises would lead to a changed life, one of goodness and love and holiness, to the complete living of our call and election. Perhaps it was a grace received on our first Communion day or wedding day. Perhaps it was a silent movement of our soul or an invitation of grace, received when someone had given us their time or been there for us when no one else was around. A sunset, a baby's smile, a funeral, our child's graduation, a quiet morning working in the garden, a prayer meeting, Eucharistic adoration.... God can move in our lives even in the most unexpected places. Take a moment to remember these times, to "scrapbook" them mentally. What was the invitation? What was the gift? What was the beauty of those moments? We are, indeed, given everything we need for a life of godliness, if we remember these precious treasures and "very great promises."

How quickly I forget, my Lord, your visits in my life. Impress on my heart and burn into my soul the vision of your face, the memory of your words to me . . . to me.

Broken for Love of Others

Then he took a loaf of bread, and when he had given thanks, he broke it and gave it to them, saying, "This is my body, which is given for you. Do this in remembrance of me." And he did the same with the cup after supper, saying, "This cup that is poured out for you is the new covenant in my blood."

LK 22:19–20

•—•••—•

At Mass—the eucharistic sacrifice, the loving last meal of Jesus celebrated again and again as the agape, the self-giving love, of the Christian community—we are there for each other. I remember being told on the day we practiced for our first Communion, "Don't look around. If I catch any of you looking around. . . ." I forget the consequences of this offense, but it was enough to keep me from looking around during Mass for years to come. Lately, however, I've come to question the wisdom of this advice. Though it may be appropriate for second graders to curtail their distraction and not look around at Mass, it may not be wise advice for adults. I would say, "Look around the next time you go to Mass. You are there for others. You are there for the world." When the priest comes to the words of consecration listen carefully. "This is my body," he says. The words of Jesus. We are called to say to one another: *This is my body, laid on the altar with Christ, broken for love of you, given over to your service, transformed by loving kindness.*

Jesus, each Sunday I witness again true love, I receive anew Love made flesh, I am shaped once more by your love, a love that is out of this world. Each week help me start afresh to give myself to others in loving service.

We Are Christ's Body

When it was evening on that day, the first day of the week, and the doors of the house where the disciples had met were locked for fear of the Jews, Jesus came and stood among them and said, "Peace be with you." After he said this, he showed them his hands and his side. Then the disciples rejoiced when they saw the Lord. Jesus said to them again, "Peace be with you. As the Father has sent me, so I send you." When he had said this, he breathed on them and said to them, "Receive the Holy Spirit. If you forgive the sins of any, they are forgiven them; if you retain the sins of any, they are retained."

JN 20:19–23

——◆·◆·◆——

Jesus knew what it was to be sent. He—completely and eagerly obedient—was sent to live among us. He healed, loved, and blessed us. He relaxed in our company. He spent his days preaching, forgiving, and teaching us to pray. He faced the utter finality of the darkness of death. Now he was sending his disciples—once fragile and afraid, now boldly transformed—to continue his work. Our deepest meaning, our essence as Church is this belonging to Christ who has named us friends. It is this being sent into the world as his body, this having been brought into existence by the Eucharist and transformed by the fire of the Spirit.

Lord, in all the struggles your Church suffers today, help us remember we are more than a group of self-appointed people who have decided to follow you. We are the body of Christ. We have been chosen and sent, loved and forgiven by you to whom we belong forever. Amen.

Sabbath Space

At that time Jesus went through the grainfields on the sabbath; his disciples were hungry, and they began to pluck heads of grain and to eat. When the Pharisees saw it, they said to him, "Look, your disciples are doing what is not lawful to do on the sabbath." He said to them, "Have you not read what David did when he and his companions were hungry? He entered the house of God and ate the bread of the Presence, which it was not lawful for him or his companions to eat.... But if you had known what this means, 'I desire mercy and not sacrifice,' you would not have condemned the guiltless. For the Son of Man is lord of the sabbath."

MT 12:1–4, 7–8

◆ • • • ◆

God gave the Hebrew people the law to keep holy the Sabbath, so they would remember and reflect on their special covenant relationship with God, who had delivered them from slavery and given them rest. The Sabbath precept, which prepares for the Sunday of the new and eternal covenant, is an indelible expression of our relationship with God. Sunday has been kept sacred by the Church because it commemorates the day of the Lord's resurrection. For centuries this day was also preserved from work because human dignity requires appropriate rest and leisure. The true meaning of work can only appear when it is alternated with rest. For some of us, the harried pace of life has blurred Sunday into any other day of the week, except that people go to church. Why not establish a Sunday ritual that will help make the whole day express the joy of your relationship with God? It could be a walk, a time of prayer, family time together, a special meal, a slowed down pace after supper, an hour of freedom from the TV or Internet. For your own sake, carve out some Sabbath space for you and God. The length of time doesn't matter as much as your desire to honor the Lord's covenant with us and his mercy in setting us free and giving us rest.

My Lord, how my heart longs for spaces of Sabbath rest. Help me cherish these sacred moments of reverent rest with you.

Running the Race

As for me, I am already being poured out as a libation, and the time of my departure has come. I have fought the good fight, I have finished the race, I have kept the faith. From now on there is reserved for me the crown of righteousness, which the Lord, the righteous judge, will give me on that day, and not only to me but also to all who have longed for his appearing.

2 Tim 4:6–8

————◆ ◆ · ◆ ◆————

Paul the Apostle. Teresa of Ávila. John of the Cross. Francis of Assisi. Elizabeth Ann Seton. John Paul II. Mother Teresa. These individuals not only ran the race, they believed that this race was the only race worth running: the race laid out by the life, death, and resurrection of Christ Jesus. It is marked by his life, and culminates in the mystery of his—and our—death and resurrection. On the way we are accompanied by the Spirit and fed by the Lord's Body in the Eucharist.

Once when reading a magazine as I waited in a doctor's office, I saw beautiful things. A Christian musician was grieving at the death of his child, and in his pain still believed. A politician's wife forgave her husband's affair in order to keep the family together. A lieutenant colonel started a scholarship fund for the children of soldiers killed in Iraq. They too are running the race. What people do *you* know who are racing on the way of Christ Jesus? How can you support them? Urge them on? Applaud them?

What a parade, dear Lord, is yours. Your people are everywhere in the world surprising everyone with their generosity, forgiveness, valor, and selfless charity. Help me to strengthen them, to cheer them on their way.

Beautiful Lives

Again he entered the synagogue, and a man was there who had a withered hand. They watched him to see whether he would cure him on the sabbath, so that they might accuse him. And he said to the man who had the withered hand, "Come forward." Then he said to them, "Is it lawful to do good or to do harm on the sabbath, to save life or to kill?" But they were silent. He looked around at them with anger; he was grieved at their hardness of heart and said to the man, "Stretch out your hand." He stretched it out, and his hand was restored. The Pharisees went out and immediately conspired with the Herodians against him, how to destroy him.

Mk 3:1–6

— • • • • —

This Gospel reading is about broken hearts. Jesus was grieved, saddened, heartbroken at the Pharisees' hardness of heart. The saints truly know what this means. They know that when we shut God out of our lives, not only are *our* hearts broken, but so also is *God's*. The saints thirsted for the opportunity to be with God in the same way a person in love desires to please their loved one. Whatever their age or vocation—mothers or fathers, kings or queens, religious, priests, or popes, doctors, children or young adults—every aspect of their day was filled with Jesus. They felt Jesus gazing on them, calling them, loving them, and even wanting to love others through them. The beauty of their lives attracted others. They gave God their voice to speak his words, their hands and feet to serve others, their eyes to reflect God's love and care to all whom they met. On the physical level, clogged arteries can lead to heart attacks and death. On the spiritual level, we may need to unblock our spiritual arteries. Let us arouse our love, stoke the fires of devotion, read the word of God, and receive God's grace in the sacraments to keep our hearts soft and open to receive the gift of God.

Lord, set my heart on fire!

Build Others Up

Blessed are the meek, for they will inherit the earth. . . .

Jesus called them to him and said, "You know that the rulers of the Gentiles lord it over them, and their great ones are tyrants over them. It will not be so among you; but whoever wishes to be great among you must be your servant, and whoever wishes to be first among you must be your slave; just as the Son of Man came not to be served but to serve, and to give his life a ransom for many."

MT 5:5; 20:25–28

◆ · · · ◆

Meek people don't make demands. Jesus is not speaking here of those who are naturally meek-tempered or weak-willed. Jesus is referring to people who are not controlled by their unconscious needs for power, control, security, affection, comfort, and esteem. When an event triggers their hidden agendas, they have learned to step back and seize the opportunity to break the cycle of anger and frustration. How? People and events can trigger all of us, and if we aren't careful, the way we react betrays that we are indeed "full of ourselves." Meek people have learned to let go and empty themselves of their addictive needs. They have discovered that they are much more than a good name, a new car, the latest gadget, a promotion, a relationship. They have learned to see themselves from the perspective of God's watchful presence. Just as God builds them up, so they become persons who return good for evil with a view to build others up, to re-create a situation, person, or relationship. They become meek because they are emptied of self-conceit.

Catch me, Lord, when I am becoming too full of myself. Catch me by surprise and attract me to the beauty of a meek life.

See with the Eyes
of the Heart

When the Son of Man comes in his glory . . . he
will sit upon his glorious throne, and all the
nations will be assembled before him. . . . Then
the king will say to those on his right, "Come,
you who are blessed by my Father. Inherit the
kingdom prepared for you from the foundation
of the world. For I was hungry and you gave me
food, I was thirsty and you gave me drink, a
stranger and you welcomed me, naked and you
clothed me, ill and you cared for me, in prison
and you visited me." . . . And the king will say to
them in reply, "Amen, I say to you, whatever you
did for one of these least brothers of mine, you
did for me."

Mt 25:31–32, 34–36, 40 (NABRE)

◆ • • • ◆

The human person is a child of God, brought
into existence by God's creative word and
immense love. Each of us, and all of us together,

share the world's resources for the period of time that is our life. Yet the problem of poverty always remains. The world is in a seemingly impossible impasse, as Jesus said: the poor you will always have with you (cf. Mt 26:11). What can break that impasse open? The prayer of the rich and the prayer of the poor, the love of the rich and the love of the poor can do so. When people can see with the eyes of the heart, they will see Christ in each other. People, whether rich or poor, can then love together. These people will become the secret makers of a new history that will hasten the coming of the kingdom of God. Jesus gives us the key in this Gospel passage, that whatever we do to others, we do to him.

May I join hands and hearts with all the people I encounter. May I think about them with compassion, speak to them in gentleness, and shoulder with them the responsibility of shaping a new way for humanity.

Lay Aside Immaturity

Wisdom has built her house,
    she has hewn her seven pillars.
She has slaughtered her animals, she has mixed
  her wine,
    she has also set her table.
She has sent out her servant-girls, she calls
    from the highest places in the town,
"You that are simple, turn in here!"
    To those without sense she says,
"Come, eat of my bread
    and drink of the wine I have mixed.
Lay aside immaturity, and live,
    and walk in the way of insight."

Prov 9:1–6

— • • • • • —

This passage makes me think of the movie *Charlie and the Chocolate Factory,* especially the line "You that are simple, turn in here! . . . Lay aside immaturity." Each of the characters in the movie becomes the victim of their foolishness or fears. But Charlie's simplicity and wisdom bring reconciliation and healing to Willy Wonka, and a better life to Charlie's beloved family. This selection from Proverbs, the treasure of God's wisdom, shows us how to live our lives in this simplicity: as intelligent and not like senseless people (see Jer 4:22). Seek the Lord, listen to him, be teachable, leave aside evil and deceit, seek peace, recognize God's will. In this way, filled with the Spirit, we will give thanks to the Father and live and mature in Christ by receiving his Body and Blood in the Eucharist.

Lord, in the chaotic confusion of life that can overwhelm me at times, guide me in the ways of perception that I may attain eternal life.

God Is Bursting into the World

Then Jesus called the twelve together and gave them power and authority over all demons and to cure diseases, and he sent them out to proclaim the kingdom of God and to heal. He said to them, "Take nothing for your journey, no staff, nor bag, nor bread, nor money—not even an extra tunic. Whatever house you enter, stay there, and leave from there. Wherever they do not welcome you, as you are leaving that town shake the dust off your feet as a testimony against them."

LK 9:1–5

◆ • • • ◆

Jesus sent the Apostles to proclaim the kingdom of God—an announcement that God is bursting into the world in the person of Jesus Christ. With this vision of reality we become grounded in our truest self: we are citizens of God's kingdom. Without this vision of reality, every stress, obstacle, or dismay we encounter can knock us off course. This faith is the light and power that nourishes our thoughts and builds true self-esteem. It gives us the confidence to believe in the sustaining love of God for us. I don't know about you, but it is so easy for me to read about faith, and at the same time so difficult to take responsibility for the way I think. My thoughts flitter here and there, getting lost in every anxiety and distortion, leading me far away from the joy of living in the kingdom of God. I shrink before the onslaught of disturbing news, fearing that negativity and not love may be the center of the universe. My thoughts can trap me and tear me away from what alone can heal me: the good news that *God is here*.

Jesus, steady my mind that I may look into each situation with the security of knowing myself a child of the Father, at home in your Kingdom. Amen.

Taken Apart and Rebuilt

In the days of his flesh, Jesus offered up prayers and supplications, with loud cries and tears, to the one who was able to save him from death, and he was heard because of his reverent submission. Although he was a Son, he learned obedience through what he suffered; and having been made perfect, he became the source of eternal salvation for all who obey him, having been designated by God a high priest according to the order of Melchizedek.

HEB 5:7–10

———— • ◦ • ————

We all know the wise advice: "Practice makes perfect." If we study hard, we can get a perfect score on a test. If we pay attention to detail and have a creative vision, we can execute the perfect project. If we are careful who we hire, we can create the perfect team. If we do things right and avoid any misstep, we'll climb the corporate ladder. If we read the right books, we'll raise perfect kids.

Perfection creates a lot of pressure. In the end, it's an illusion. I am grateful I learned early on through serious sickness that real "perfection" comes through suffering: through darkness faced, disaster overcome, temptation endured, sickness surmounted or surrendered to. When one has been taken apart and rebuilt through this process, then "perfection" does roll off our fingers: a perfection that is received. I don't need to achieve or accomplish anything to be perfect. I only need to surrender to what God is doing in me and through me in the world. It may look "perfect" according to others, or it may look like a complete disaster, as did the crucifixion of Jesus. In either case, as long as God is glorified, it is perfectly fine with me.

Accomplish your will in me, my God. Right now I embrace whatever your will may be. With all my heart I desire it. Amen.

Also by Kathryn J. Hermes, FSP

Reclaim Regret: How God Heals Life's Disappointments

Encounter the healing love of Jesus through scriptural prayer, stories, meditations, and reflections, and experience for yourself that God can transform even our deepest regrets and bring us freedom.

0-8198-6513-3   192 pages $14.95 U.S.

Jesus: Mercy from God's Heart

Beautiful reflections on the merciful love of Jesus as shown in the Gospels, the devotion of the saints, and in the stories of people today. Includes prayers to the Sacred Heart, Divine Mercy, and other prayers of intercession for mercy.

0-8198-4015-7   144 pages $7.95 U.S.

Surviving Depression: A Catholic Approach

A reassuring approach to living through depression, which has helped thousands of readers. Translated into twelve languages.

0-8198-7225-3   192 pages $14.95 U.S.

Also in the Just a Minute Series

Meditations for Deeper Trust

by Sr. Kathryn J. Hermes, FSP

Fifty scriptural meditations to help you surrender everything into the hands of Jesus and be secure in his love.

0-8198-4978-2   112 pages $5.95 U.S.

Meditations to Grow in Self-Esteem

by Sr Marie Paul Curley, FSP

Fifty scriptural meditations to improve self-esteem by coming to truly believe in God's great love for you.

0-8198-4986-3   112 pages $5.95 U.S.

Pauline
BOOKS & MEDIA

A mission of the Daughters of St. Paul

As apostles of Jesus Christ,
evangelizing today's world:

We are CALLED to holiness
by God's living Word and Eucharist.

We COMMUNICATE the Gospel message
through our lives and through all
available forms of media.

We SERVE the Church
by responding to the hopes and needs
of all people with the Word of God,
in the spirit of St. Paul.

For more information visit www.pauline.org.

BOOKS & MEDIA

The Daughters of St. Paul operate book and media centers at the following addresses. Visit, call, or write the one nearest you today, or find us at www.paulinestore.org.

CALIFORNIA
3908 Sepulveda Blvd, Culver City, CA 90230   310-397-8676
3250 Middlefield Road, Menlo Park, CA 94025   650-562-7060

FLORIDA
145 S.W. 107th Avenue, Miami, FL 33174   305-559-6715

HAWAII
1143 Bishop Street, Honolulu, HI 96813   808-521-2731

ILLINOIS
172 North Michigan Avenue, Chicago, IL 60601   312-346-4228

LOUISIANA
4403 Veterans Memorial Blvd, Metairie, LA 70006   504-887-7631

MASSACHUSETTS
885 Providence Hwy, Dedham, MA 02026   781-326-5385

MISSOURI
9804 Watson Road, St. Louis, MO 63126   314-965-3512

NEW YORK
115 E. 29th Street, New York City, NY 10016   212-754-1110

SOUTH CAROLINA
243 King Street, Charleston, SC 29401   843-577-0175

TEXAS
No book center; for parish exhibits or outreach evangelization, contact: 210-569-0500, or SanAntonio@paulinemedia.com, or P.O. Box 761416, San Antonio, TX 78245

VIRGINIA
1025 King Street, Alexandria, VA 22314   703-549-3806

CANADA
3022 Dufferin Street, Toronto, ON M6B 3T5   416-781-9131